Philip Hewitt

QUEST FOR A FATHER

Illustrations: Jette Jørgensen

Philip Hewitt:
Quest for a Father
Teen Readers, Level 3

Series editor: Ulla Malmmose

© 1998 by Philip Hewitt and
ASCHEHOUG/ALINEA, Copenhagen
ISBN Denmark 87-23-90176-4
www.easyreader.dk

Printed in Denmark by
Sangill Grafisk Produktion, Holme Olstrup

About the author

Philip Hewitt studied German and French at Oxford and taught both languages in Britain for two years at the Royal Merchant Navy School near Reading, after which he was prepared to give up teaching for ever!

In 1970 he moved to Germany with his German wife and young daughter, first to Hanover, where he became a teacher of English, then to Stuttgart, where he worked as an editor in the Modern Languages department of a large German publishing house before becoming a freelance translator and teacher in 1977.

Since then he has written several English textbooks and readers, mostly published in Germany. He teaches English at all levels, including University (where he does a weekly seminar on Business English "just for fun").

His leisure interests and hobbies include reading, writing, restoring classic cars (like Miss Moggy in this story!) and trying to win the weekly quiz at the local "Irish Pub", where he got the idea for this story.

Vicky

1

Vicky was only fourteen years old when her mother was killed in a car crash.

Vicky was in the car with her. One moment they had been driving back home to Coventry one evening after a visit to some friends of her mother's in Kidderminster, the next moment there was a loud bang, and the car *swerved* out of control across all three lanes of the *motorway*, up the grass bank at the side and into a field. One of the tyres had burst. Vicky could not remember much about the accident: the loud bang as the tyre burst, the bright green of the grass in the car's *headlights*, the *distorted music* on the cassette as the car turned over once, twice, three times. She remembered her mother saying: "Oh God, no!" or something like that. She remembered nothing else until she woke up in hospital the next day.

Vicky had been wearing her seat-belt, her mother had not. She had always said she felt uncomfortable with the belt on. It was three days before Vicky was well enough to be told the bad news: her mother Janet was dead. It was a terrible shock for Vicky. She cried quietly - for hours, it seemed. Everyone at the hospital was very kind to her, but she was still suffering from shock. Friends came and visited her: her school friends, her mother's friends. No one else, because Vicky was *an only child* who had been brought up by her mother. Whenever Vicky

---

to swerve, to move to the side suddenly
motorway, big road for cars with two to three lanes
headlight, main lamp at the front of a car
distorted music, when the tape in a cassette moves faster or slower than normal, the music is distorted
an only child, a child with no brothers or sisters

had asked about her father, her mother had said: "Oh **him**! We don't need **him**, love! He doesn't even know that you *exist*. We manage fine without a man in the house, don't we? Just the two of us. You don't need a father. You've got **me**!"

Now she had nobody. Nobody except her grandmother, who lived in South Wales and had been too ill herself to visit Vicky in hospital.

Vicky's seat-belt had saved her life, but it had also broken her *collar-bone* and four of her *ribs*. Her face had been badly cut by glass from the broken windscreen, and when the nurses took the *bandages* off her face, Vicky cried again. There was a long, red cut across her left *cheek* from ear to *chin*, and the doctors had had to put ten stitches in it.

"Don't worry too much, love," a young doctor had said. "We can do something about the *scar* later. You're lucky to be *alive*." She knew that, but it didn't help much.

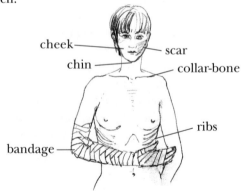

---

to exist, to live, to be living
alive, living, not dead

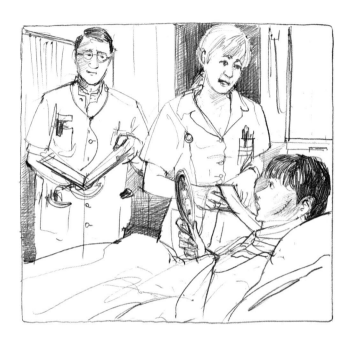

* * *

2

Three weeks later, when Vicky was well enough to leave hospital, her grandmother came up to Coventry from Wales to fetch her home.

The small flat in the tower block where Vicky had spent all her life seemed strangely empty without her mother, but she knew she would be leaving it soon. She would be going to live with her grandmother in Wales. Mrs Griffiths had only come to Coventry for a few days to help Vicky pack her things, to sell most of the *furniture* and to *arrange* for a *charity shop* to pick up Vicky's mother's clothing. "Unless, of course, there's any clothing of Janet's that would fit you, Vicky," she had said. " - You're a big girl for your age."

Vicky shook her head: "No, Gran. Mum's things wouldn't fit me yet. They don't even *suit* me." She looked at the *wardrobe* full of clothes, clothes which her mother had loved to wear, and shook her head again. "No. Oxfam can have them all. They'll make some money to help poor people in the Third World. Mum would have wanted that."

"All right, love. I'll finish packing the other things. Perhaps you could pack your mother's private things in this box. We'll have to look through them some time, but not just yet."

---

furniture, a bed, a cupboard and a table are pieces of furniture
to arrange, to organize
charity shop, shop run by an organization like Oxfam where gifts of old clothes, books etc. are sold to make money to help poor people in Britain or the Third World
to suit, to look good on s.o. (clothing)
wardrobe, a cupboard to store clothing in

Vicky opened the *drawers* of her mother's desk and put the things into the box. Notebooks, old diaries, letters, papers... Her mother had never thrown anything away. Right at the back of the last drawer was a big *envelope* with the letter "B" on it. What could it mean? The envelope was *sealed*, so Vicky just put it in the box with the other things and thought no more about it.

The people from Oxfam came later in the afternoon and took all Jan's clothes away. They were very *sympathetic*, very friendly, very pleased. Most of Jan's clothes were quite new and had not been worn much. "Thank you very much, Mrs Griffiths," the young man said to Vicky's grandmother. "The money we get will give a lot of people a chance to live happier lives."

Vicky turned away and walked into the empty kitchen. She wanted to be alone. She wanted to think. Happier lives? She was only fourteen. Had she had a happy life so far? Had her mother lived a happy life? She had died at the age of forty-three, which seemed old to Vicky. Her grandmother was sixty-seven - *ancient*! What must it be like to die suddenly in the middle of your life, just when you were not expecting it? Just when you thought you might have a chance to start a new life? What was it they said? "Life begins at forty." Jan had never married, but Vicky knew that she had had boyfriends who had wanted to live with her - even marry her, perhaps. But Jan had

---

drawer, part of a cupboard or desk, a wooden box with a handle to be pulled out and pushed back in
envelope, letters are put into envelopes to be mailed
to seal, to close tight, in the old days letters were sealed with wax
sympathetic, understanding
ancient, very old, like in Ancient Greece

been too independent. She had been a teacher with a good job that she had enjoyed. She had been a good mother to Vicky. Vicky tried hard to imagine what it would have been like to have a man around the house, a father, even a *step-father*, but she couldn't.

Now she was going to live with her grandmother. Vicky had spent a few weeks each year during the school holidays at her grandmother's house in the small South Wales *border* town of Usk, where she had moved after her husband had been killed in a coal-mine accident. Vicky had found Usk a very quiet place compared to Coventry. The nearest disco was in Pontypool, and in the evenings all the young people seemed to leave Usk by bus or by car, looking for fun in places which were only a quarter of the size of the town where Vicky had *grown up*. She would miss Coventry. She would miss her school and her friends. What would life be like in her new *surroundings*? She would soon know.

Vicky slept in her old bedroom for the last time that night. She had taken all the pictures and posters off the walls and packed her few books and CDs. The room seemed strangely empty, and she had a strange dream. Not really a dream - it was a *nightmare*. She was walking down a long, dark tunnel. There was a light at the end of the tunnel. As she walked, the light got brighter. Now she could see someone standing at the end of the tunnel. It was a man. He was holding out his arms towards

---

step-father, not the real father, a man married to the mother who helps to raise the children from the first marriage
border, political line separating two countries
to grow up, a child grows up to become an adult
surroundings, neighbourhood, area you live
nightmare, bad dream

her. She wanted to walk faster, but something was holding her back. The man was waving to her as if he wanted her to hurry, but suddenly she couldn't move. Something was pulling her back. Why didn't the man come down the tunnel to help her? The end of the tunnel seemed to be getting further and further away. The man seemed to be getting smaller, too. He stopped waving and just stood there, his hands at his sides: a dark shadow against the bright light from outside. Then even the light from outside began to *fade*. A voice behind Vicky said: "We don't need **him**! He doesn't even know that you **exist**. We manage fine without him, don't we? Just the two of us. You don't need **him**, Vicky. You've got **me**!" Vicky felt her mother's hand on her shoulder. She gave a cry - and awoke.

The early May sun was shining through the window. Her grandmother was shaking her shoulder gently. "Wake up, love! It's nearly eight! Did I frighten you?"

"No, Gran. It was only a bad dream I was having."

"Get up, then. Breakfast's ready. The *removal van* will be here at nine."

---

to fade, here: to get darker
removal van, a truck to transport furniture on moving day

3

The removal men put the few boxes and pieces of furniture into the van and drove off. The flat was empty now. Vicky took a last look round, remembering the many happy times she and Jan had had there: birthday parties, Christmases with friends of hers and Jan's. Even as an only child she had never felt as lonely as she felt now.

"Come on, love," said Mrs Griffiths, picking up their bags. "It's time to go now. The flat's empty, but you can take your memories with you." Vicky said a secret goodbye to the empty rooms and walked down to the car with her grandmother.

The sun shone almost all the way to South Wales. Mrs Griffiths was a good driver. After her accident, Vicky was a bit nervous about travelling by car, but she felt quite safe in her grandmother's little Mini as it *overtook* the slow lorries on the motorway from Coventry to the South West. They left the motorway near Gloucester and drove through the Forest of Dean towards South Wales. Mrs Griffiths talked to Vicky about their new life.

"I'm sure you'll settle down well in Usk, dear. The local school is very good, and there are *plenty* of young people of your age."

There were more clouds in the sky as they left the Forest of Dean, and as they drove down the long hill towards the old bridge over the River Wye at Monmouth it began to rain. When they crossed the bridge, they would be in Wales. Vicky asked her grandmother a question that had been worrying her. "I won't have to learn Welsh at school, will I, Gran?"

---

to overtake, to pass a car on the road
plenty, many, much, a lot of

Mrs Griffiths laughed. "No, love! Not now. A few years ago, yes. Not many people in Usk speak Welsh, though you can learn it at evening classes, of course. You'll be too close to the English border. It's not a very Welsh part of Wales."

They drove on through Gwent. The rain got worse.

"Does it always rain so much in May?" Vicky asked.

"Not usually, dear. But we've had a dry spring, and the farmers have been waiting for a little rain."

Of course. It was a farming area. No big towns. No discos. Nothing exciting. Vicky put her hand up to her cheek and felt the hard line of the scar and the *bumps*

---

bump, s.th. sticking out from an even surface

where the stitches had been. Already she thought she knew what her *nickname* at her new school would be: "Scarface".

But she was wrong. The other kids called her "*Brummie*" because of her Birmingham *accent*. They knew what had happened to her and were very kind to her. She soon made new friends and began to feel at home. Mrs Griffiths was pleased. She hoped her granddaughter would like her new home. Mrs Griffiths had not liked her daughter Janet's independent life-style. Jan had been a very independent young woman. She had gone to university and become a teacher in Coventry. Mr and Mrs Griffiths had expected her to stay single or to marry. Instead, at the age of twenty-eight, she had *become pregnant*.

When Jan had told her parents that she was pregnant, Mr and Mrs Griffiths had been shocked. As *working-class* people in a small mining village, they had always lived a hard life, and *strict* religious and moral standards had been part of that life. To the Griffiths, the idea of bringing up a child as a single parent had seemed wrong. They had asked their daughter about "the father", but Jan had only laughed: "Never mind about him! We women only need men for one thing. Marriage was made for men, Mum! Sorry, Dad! Washing his clothes, cooking his

---

nickname, a made-up name used among friends or family
Brummie, nickname for s.o. from Birmingham
accent, the way a person pronounces words according to the region he or she lives in
to become pregnant, to expect a child to be born
working-class, people working at a factory are working-class
strict, following clear rules that are taken very seriously

meals, listening to him *snoring* in bed every night! I don't need marriage! I've got a good job and good friends. I want this child and I can bring it up by myself. I hope it's a girl. Girls are easier to look after than boys!"

She had got her wish. She had called her daughter Victoria, perhaps because she saw single *parenthood* as a victory of women over men. And she had done her job well. Vicky was a fine girl. But now Mrs Griffiths would have to take over from Jan, and again there was no man in the house. How she wished her husband Terry was still alive!

---

to snore, to make noises through one's nose or mouth while sleeping
parenthood, being a mother or father

4

A year passed. Vicky lost her Birmingham accent and the other kids stopped calling her "Brummie". She began to do well at school. The doctors at Nevill Hall Hospital in
5 Abergavenny did a wonderful job on her scar, so that only a thin line was left. Vicky began to lead a normal life again.

But Mrs Griffiths had a *weak* heart. She had been ill *several* times over the past couple of years, and a few days
10 after Vicky's fifteenth birthday, she had a heart attack and had to go into hospital for a few days. Vicky stayed with the family of Anne Matthews, her best friend, and one evening a social worker from the *Youth Welfare Office* visited her.

15 The woman was very sympathetic, but the message was clear: Vicky would have to look after her grandmother when she came out of hospital, and if Mrs Griffiths' health did not *improve*, Vicky might have to be placed with *foster parents* or even put in a children's home. Very
20 *tactfully*, the social worker asked Vicky if she knew anything about her father. Vicky told her that she knew nothing about him. "Mum always said we didn't need him. She said he didn't even know that I existed."

---

weak, not strong
several, a few, one or two, a small number of things
Youth Welfare Office, children that have no parents or only one parent are looked after by the Youth Welfare Office
to improve, to make better, to get better
foster parents, a married couple that takes care of a child that has no parents
tactful, not wishing to hurt s.o.'s feelings

"I see," was all the social worker said. She left soon afterwards.

The idea of going into a children's home worried Vicky. She was happy living with her grandmother. In three years she would be eighteen and could do what she liked. Three years in a home, or with foster parents! If only she knew more about her father! Who was he? Was he still alive? Did he really not know that she existed? Would he be pleased if he knew?

She was still thinking about her father when she went to bed that night. And that night she had the same dream about walking down a long, dark tunnel towards a shadowy figure at the end of it, a figure that seemed to *disappear* as she heard her dead mother's words yet again: "We don't need **him**!" But this was not true any more. She had no mother. Why shouldn't she have a father?

After school the next day she went *straight* home, took the *stepladder* from the kitchen, walked upstairs to the *landing* and climbed up into the *loft*. Over in one corner was the box with Jan's personal papers that Vicky had packed over a year before. She carried it down to her bedroom and began to hunt.

There was a *bundle* of old diaries. With *trembling* fingers she pulled out the diary for the year before she had been born. The *entries* in the diary were not very long,

---

to disappear, to go away
straight, directly
stepladder, landing, loft, see illustration, page 18
bundle, number of things placed one on top of the other
to tremble, to shake nervously
entry, a paragraph, here: in the diary

just times and places, appointments, meetings, concerts Jan had gone to, names of private pupils she had taught in her free time. Details of holidays and trips. Vicky looked quickly down the pages, leaving out most of the details, searching for something which her mother had taught her, at the age of 13, to put in her diary every month. There it was! A *tiny* "x" in red pencil. Vicky quickly turned over three pages of the diary. There it was again, on the fourth page, after the fourth week. A tiny red "x", after twenty-eight days. May, June and again on 12th July.

The entry for 15th July, just after the school summer term had probably ended, read: "Left for Ireland today. Hooray!". Then just places, times of buses and trains. Then, on 24th July a single *enigmatic* letter: "B". And again on each of the next three days. Then nothing but place names until 15th August, when the entry read: "Home (worst luck). Wonderful holiday!"

No "x" anywhere during the month of August. Vicky moved on to early September. Nothing. Then, in the middle of September: "Saw Dr. M., 3.15. No doubt about it! Victoria, *here we go!*"

Before Vicky could stop them, two fat tears rolled down her cheeks and onto the pages of the diary. She suddenly felt like a thief, a burglar, only she had not broken into a house. She had broken into a secret past - her mother's past, **her own past**. Now she knew what she wanted to know. Or part of what she needed to know.

She quickly looked through the other papers. Old

---

tiny, very small
enigmatic, puzzling
here we go! exclamation when starting s.th.

bills, old birthday cards, several of which she had given her mother herself. A few more tears, then on with the *search*. Nothing. Nothing but a large sealed envelope with one letter on it: "B".

Vicky could feel her heart beating as she opened the envelope. There were three more envelopes inside. They had Irish *stamps* on them and had never been opened. Vicky arranged them in order of the date on the *postmark*. The first two had been sent to her mother at an address in Coventry that Vicky had never heard of. The third had been sent by the Post Office to the flat where Vicky had grown up. So her mother must have moved house before Vicky was born. The postmark was 19th December. It was a bigger envelope. A Christmas card, perhaps?

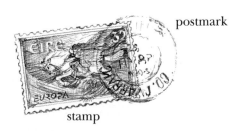

Three letters from Ireland which Jan had never opened, never read, never answered. Were they letters from the same "B" who had appeared four times in Jan's diary? There was no sender's address on the envelope. She would have to open one of the letters.

---

search, a very thorough look for s.th.

Vicky's hands trembled as she opened the first envelope, postmarked 17th September. She pulled out a piece of paper, a page torn from a child's school exercise book. The *handwriting* was difficult to read, but the sender's address was in the top right-hand corner, exactly where she herself had been taught to put it at school.

Vicky *lowered* her eyes to the beginning of the letter and slowly, *unbelievingly* read the words her mother had never read. The letter began: "My Dearest Darling Jan..."

Vicky could not go on. It seemed like *sacrilege* to read a love letter written to her mother. She would read it later, perhaps. Perhaps not.

She put the box back into the loft and kept only the diary and the letters. At least she now had a name, an address, something to go on, perhaps someone *to turn to* in need. Should she show the letters to her grandmother? No. Gran was too ill for a surprise like this! Vicky would have to keep the secret to herself. She would have to wait and see.

---

handwriting, words written by hand
to lower, to move downwards
unbelievingly, not believing
sacrilege, breaking a religious taboo
to turn to s.o., to ask s.o. for help

5

When Mrs Griffiths came out of hospital, she was still very weak, and Vicky would not let her do any of the *housework*. The social services brought her "meals on wheels" while Vicky was at school, and slowly Mrs Griffiths' health improved.

A week after her grandmother's return, Vicky felt ready to read the first letter which Brendan - that was the name at the bottom of the letter - had written to her mother almost sixteen years before.

My Dearest Darling Jan,

I know you asked me not to write to you, but I have been so worried about you that I got your address from the hotel.

I know we agreed that we should not *continue* our relationship, that it was just a holiday affair, but I can't stop thinking about you. It is now over a month since you left Ireland, so I want to ask you just one thing: are you all right? You know what I mean. We were very silly not to take any of the usual *precautions*, and I will never *forgive* myself if I have done anything to *spoil* your life.

As you know, I am just a simple man, but you can believe me when I say I love you and cannot understand **why** we cannot meet again and *get to know* each other

---

housework, cooking, cleaning etc. is housework
to continue, to go on with
precaution, method to avoid an accident
to forgive, to pardon
to spoil, to change a situation into a bad situation
to get to know s.o., to meet and make friends with s.o.

properly. What is so wrong about a teacher marrying a farmer? I would even join you in England if I didn't have to look after my old mother and younger brothers and sisters. Or you could come and live over here in Ireland. You said you loved the country and the people. There would be jobs for teachers at the National Schools in Kenmare or Killarney.

I'm sure we could be happy together. Won't you please think about it and write soon? I won't be able to sleep properly until I know that everything is all right with you.

I love you and *pray* for you every night,

Brendan

Vicky carefully put the letter back in the envelope. She closed her eyes and tried to imagine what her life might have been like if her mother had married this man.

She saw herself growing up on a small farm somewhere in Ireland instead of in a small fifth-floor flat in Coventry. She saw herself feeding the *chickens, milking* the cow, walking to school hand-in-hand with a younger brother or sister through the gentle Irish rain. She saw herself in a white dress at her *first Communion* in a tiny, *candle-lit* village church with many boys and girls of her

---

to pray, to speak to God
chicken, hen, bird that provides eggs to eat and lives on a farm
to milk, to get milk from a cow
first Communion, Catholics have their first Communion at the age of ten when they first receive bread symbolizing Christ's body
candle-lit, lit by candles

own age. She saw herself learning to ride a pony, a smiling father at her side making sure she didn't fall off and hurt herself. Then she stopped thinking. Thinking about what might have been was no good! If she did anything, it would have to be something practical.

Vicky looked at the address: Brendan Sullivan, Long House Farm, Templenoe, Nr. Kenmare, *Co.* Kerry. Where on earth was County Kerry? She would look it up in the big *atlas* in the school *library* the next day.

Should she write? Would he still be living there after sixteen years? No, a letter would be too impersonal. He might no longer be living at the old address. She would go to Ireland and find him herself! In the summer holidays, perhaps. But what if Gran would not let her go? She would go anyway. And if Gran's heart got any worse, she would go before the Youth Welfare people could put her in a children's home!

There and then she decided to tell her grandmother nothing. It was too big a secret. Too much depended on it. She would only tell her best friend Anne Matthews. Anne was in her class at school, and they had shared all their secrets almost from the day Vicky had arrived in Usk.

Vicky picked up the phone and rang Anne's number: "Hello? Anne? Are you doing anything this evening. I've got to talk to you. Yes, it's very important, but I can't talk on the phone. Gran will be back from the doctor's any minute, and you know she doesn't like me using the phone. Seven-thirty at Luigi's? Fine!"

Co., short for county
atlas, a collection of maps in a book
library, a place where a lot of books are stored for people to read and borrow

6

"You mean you really know who your father is?" whispered Anne excitedly.

They were sitting at a small table in a little Italian café in Usk's main street. The café was full, and the radio was playing loud pop music, but they spoke in whispers, like *conspirators*.

conspirator, a person sharing a secret with s.o. or planning to commit a crime

"Well, I've got the address where he was living when my mother met him. It's a little place called Templenoe near Kenmare in County Kerry."

"That's in the south-west. It's a beautiful part of Ireland. We went there three years ago. I think we've still got a map at home. I'll look for it and lend you it. But surely a lot must have happened in sixteen years, Vicky. He probably got married years ago and might have six children by now! He won't be pleased to know he fathered a child all those years ago - nor will his wife!"

"I know," said Vicky. "But I've got to find out! You've no idea what it's like, Anne. If Gran's heart condition gets worse, they'll put me with foster parents or in a children's home. I don't want that!" Vicky was silent for a few moments, then she looked Anne straight in the eyes and asked: "Will you come with me to Ireland, Anne? In the summer holidays? You've been there before. You know your way about."

"I don't know," said Anne *thoughtfully*. "I'm not sure my parents would let me, even if the two of us went."

"But you're nine months older than me. You'll be sixteen in August. Surely they'd let you go?"

"Maybe. But I'll have to think about it, Vicky. I'm still not sure you're doing the right thing. Why don't you just show the Youth Welfare people the letter and let **them** find your father?"

"Because I don't want him to find out about me that way. Official letters and perhaps even a court case! That would be a fine way for a daughter to introduce herself to her father, wouldn't it! I don't want *to get him into trou-*

---

thoughtful, thinking about s.th. while speaking
to get s.o. into trouble, to put a person in a bad situation

ble, Anne. I don't want money from him. I'm not even sure I want him to help me. I might not even like him when I meet him!"

"Aren't you being a bit romantic about it all, Vicky? Let's be practical. If this Brendan really **is** your father, he might be able to offer you a home, or he might not. But he'll be a complete stranger to you, and you to him! Would it be fair to go over to Ireland and *confront* him with a part of his past that he may have forgotten or may not want to remember? He'll be over forty now, and *Irishmen* don't usually stay single into their forties - unless they become *priests*. If we just arrive at his door one morning, we might ruin a happy marriage."

"I don't want to do it like that, Anne. I just want to **see** him. To get to know him. To find out what he's like. Surely you can understand that?"

"Of course I can **understand** it, Vicky. I'm lucky. I've had two parents all my life. But I'm not sure how I'd feel if I found out I had an older sister or brother. My feelings towards my father would certainly change! I think Mum and Dad want to go to south-west Ireland again this year. I wonder if I could invite you to come with us?"

Vicky gave a cry of *delight*. "That would be wonderful, Anne. It'd *solve* all my problems if I could go to Ireland with you. Perhaps we could take a trip to Kenmare on our own. Would you come with me to Templenoe, Anne?"

---

to confront, to face a person with news
Irishman, a person from Ireland
priest, a man working full-time in the church
to ruin, here: to spoil, to break up
delight, joy, happiness, pleasure
to solve, to find the answer to a problem

"Of course I would. But don't start making plans before I've asked Mum and Dad if you can come with us!"

7

Mr and Mrs Matthews thought it would be a very good idea to take Vicky on holiday with them. She would be good company for Anne, who was also an only child.

Mrs Griffiths thought it was a good idea, too. Her doctor had told her that she would have to go into hospital for a *by-pass* operation that summer. Perhaps she could have the operation while Vicky was away in Ireland.

During the late spring and early summer, Vicky saved every penny she could. She studied the map of Killarney District which Mr Matthews had lent her, and even found the tiny village of Templenoe. It was on the N70 road about five miles west of Kenmare and only a quarter of a mile from Kenmare River, which was over a mile wide at this point. There were high hills behind the village and on the other side of the wide river. There was even an old castle not far away.

But before she went to Ireland, Vicky would have to find out more about Brendan Sullivan. So on June 10th, Jan's birthday, she opened his second letter.

It was very short, no more than a note asking Jan to write, but inside the envelope was a colour photo. It showed a much younger Jan standing beside a tall, *dark-haired* young man. They had their arms around each other and were smiling. Behind them was a lake with a castle and blue hills in the distance. On the back Brendan had written: "Killarney Lakes, last July. How I wish you were here!"

---

by-pass, operation on the heart to let the blood flow freely
dark-haired, a person who has brown or black hair is dark-haired

So this was Brendan, her father. Vicky looked carefully at the photo for a long time and tried to imagine the man sixteen years later. He had probably been about twenty-five when the photo was taken. If he were an outdoor worker, he would not have lost his *slim, muscular* figure. His hair might be thinner now, of course, but Vicky thought she would know him when she saw him.

The weather stayed fine all June. A long, hot summer was *forecast*, and Vicky began to look forward to her holiday. She borrowed all the travel books about Ireland from the local library one after the other. The country began to *fascinate* her. She bought road maps of Wales and Ireland, and followed the route they would take:

---

slim, not fat
muscular, to have well-developed muscles
to forecast, to give information about the coming weather
to fascinate, to interest s.o. very much

across South Wales to Fishguard, then onto the ferry across the Irish Sea to Rosslare. Then along the south coast of Ireland to Kerry. They would be staying for a few days at different places, and one of those places would be Killarney, one of the country's most popular tourist areas.*

Vicky and Anne would find an excuse for an excursion to Kenmare, and they would take a bus (she hoped there was one) to Templenoe and find out what they could about Brendan Sullivan. But before their holiday there were still three weeks of school with *end-of-term* exams for which Vicky was now working hard. She would be taking her *GCSE exams* the following summer. If she did well, she would stay on at school. If not, she would have to look for a job.

The end of term came at last. Vicky did well at her exams. Mrs Griffiths was pleased, and gave her a little extra pocket money for her holiday. The date for Mrs Griffiths' operation was fixed. She would have to go into hospital for three weeks on the day before Vicky and Anne's family left for Ireland. The doctors told her that there was nothing to worry about. She would be back home at the end of August, just after Vicky got back from her holiday.

Then, just a week before the holiday, *disaster*! Anne's father fell off his bike and broke his leg. They would have to *cancel* the holiday. When Anne came round with the news, Vicky was so angry she could hardly speak. All

---

* see map, page 39
end-of-term, at the end of a school year
GCSE exams, school exams at the age of sixteen
disaster, s.th. terrible which happens
to cancel, to not do s.th. one had planned

her plans were ruined!

"I'm so sorry, Vicky," Anne said. "But it's not Dad's fault. He was looking forward to this holiday as much as we all were."

"Never mind," said Vicky at last. Despite her great *disappointment* she realized that it was nobody's fault. "I'll just have to wait a bit longer. But you must promise me something, Anne. If I decide to go to Ireland on my own, you must give me six hours' start."

Anne was shocked. "You're not thinking of running away, are you, Vicky?"

"Ask me no questions and I'll tell you no lies. Just promise!"

"OK, I promise."

An ambulance picked Mrs Griffiths up the following Friday afternoon, and Vicky, who would be staying with Anne's family again instead of going on holiday with them, promised to look after the house while Mrs Griffiths was away.

Anne and Vicky went for a long walk the next day. They talked about almost everything except Ireland, although Anne realized that Vicky was still thinking about their spoilt holiday. To take her mind off Ireland, Anne asked Vicky if she would like to go to a disco in Newport the following Saturday.

"Newport? What's wrong with the disco in Pontypool? All our friends will be there as usual."

"I just thought you might like a change," said Anne.

---

disappointment, sadness about s.th. one has wished for and which doesn't happen

"We can ask Roger and Neil to go. You know how much Neil likes you!"

Vicky thought for a moment and suddenly became very *enthusiastic* about the idea. "Why not? It'll *make a change*. Yes, let's do that."

Mrs Griffiths had her heart operation on the following Monday, but when Vicky arrived at the hospital the next day to visit her grandmother, the nurse asked her to wait outside and have a few words with the doctor first. She sat down and waited, feeling just a little worried.

"Miss Griffiths?"

---

enthusiastic, very happy, bursting with joy and excitement
to make a change, to be different, to do s.th. in a different way

Vicky jumped at the sound of her own name. She hadn't heard the doctor walk up behind her.

"Yes?"

"I'd like a few words with you. Come this way please," and he led her into his office. They sat down.

"First of all, the good news: the operation was a success. Your grandmother will make a complete *recovery* - in time."

"In time?" said Vicky. "What do you mean?"

"She's weaker than we thought. She won't be able to leave hospital for several weeks yet, and then she will have to go to a *convalescent home* for at least a month." He looked down at some papers on his desk. "I see that you have no other relatives in the area, and as you are only fifteen, the Youth Welfare Office may have to find foster parents for you until your grandmother is completely well."

"But I can look after her just as well at home, can't I?"

"I'm afraid not," said the doctor. "She'll need special care while she's here in hospital, and during *convalescence*."

Vicky felt a cold *shiver* run down her *spine*.

"There's something you haven't told me, isn't there, Doctor?"

The doctor looked down at his desk again and moved the papers around before speaking. "I'm afraid there is some not-so-good news, too. Miss Griffiths," he began.

---

recovery, getting better after an illness
convalescent home, a place where sick people can relax and recover after they leave hospital
convalescence, time of recovery after an illness
shiver, sudden coldness on the skin
spine, bones down the back from the neck to the bottom

" - Your grandmother is still *unconscious*. This sometimes happens after a heart by-pass operation. We expect her to *regain consciousness* later today. That's why we would prefer you not to see her at the moment."

"Why not?"

"She's in *intensive care*. We don't usually allow people under sixteen to visit patients in the intensive care unit. As you are her only relative, I could let you see her, of course. But you wouldn't be able to talk to her at the moment, and the visit might *distress* you." He looked down at the papers again. "Where are you living at the moment?"

"With my best friend Anne Matthews and her family. In Usk. We **were** going to go on holiday to Ireland..."

"Well, you can probably stay there for the moment, if the Matthews agree, but as you are still under eighteen, I expect the Youth Welfare Office will be in touch with you within the next few days. Can I have your telephone number at the Matthews'?"

"Telephone number?"

"So we can ring you when your grandmother's condition improves. Or perhaps you'd like to ring us?"

Vicky left the hospital feeling very *upset*. What if her grandmother didn't recover? What if she *went into a coma* and died? She couldn't stay with the Matthews forever. The Youth Welfare people would put her in a home!

Unless...

---

unconscious, not yet awake after an operation
to regain consciousness, to wake up after an operation
intensive care, a part of the hospital for seriously ill people
to distress, to make very sad
upset, nervous, distressed
to go into a coma, to lose consciousness for a long time

As she waited for the bus back to Usk, a plan began to form in her head.

During the next few days there was little change in Mrs Griffiths' condition. She regained consciousness, but was very weak. Vicky visited her in the intensive care unit twice, but the doctor had been right. The visits only distressed her. Everyone was sympathetic and *encouraged* her to look on the bright side, but Vicky was a realist. She had been close to death herself once, and she knew the signs.

---

to encourage, to influence a person to do s.th.

8

"I've got to go into Newport on the early bus, Anne," said Vicky the following Saturday. "There's something I have to do. I'll meet you at the disco at eight."

"OK," said Anne. "Roger and Neil are coming, so don't be late!" Roger was Anne's boyfriend, and Neil was very interested in Vicky.

Vicky met her friends as arranged, and they spent the evening in the usual way: dancing, drinking Coke, talking (when the music was not too loud) and enjoying themselves. Neil danced with Vicky most of the time, but at about ten o'clock she said she wanted to go outside for a bit of fresh air. Neil offered to join her, but she asked him not to. She said she wanted to be alone.

The three friends went on dancing together for a while, and the music was so good that it was only a quarter of an hour later that Neil realized Vicky had not come back yet.

"Where on earth is she?" he asked.

"Perhaps she's still outside," said Anne. "I'll go and have a look."

There were one or two other people outside the disco, but no sign of Vicky.

"Have you seen Vicky, Paul?" Anne asked one of the boys outside, who was in their class at school.

"I saw her at the station just now when I got off the train from Pontypool. I thought she was on her way home."

"On her way home? But what would she be doing at the railway station? We came by bus from Usk." Then she remembered that Vicky had taken an earlier bus.

"Did she have anything with her, Paul? Anything at all? A sports bag or a *suitcase*?"

Paul thought for a second. "Yes, she did. She had a big rucksack with her. Looked as if she was going on a trip somewhere..."

Anne left the others at the disco and ran to the station as fast as she could. There was no sign of Vicky on any of the three platforms. She checked her watch. It was exactly ten-thirty. The information desk was closed, so she walked up to one of the platform staff.

"I'm looking for a friend and I don't know where she's gone. Can you tell me which trains have left the station during the last half hour?"

"Only three, love," he said. "The 22.05 for Abergavenny, Hereford and Manchester, the 22.12 for London, Paddington and the 22.21 for Fishguard *Harbour*."

"The Irish Boat Train?"

"That's right. It was seven minutes late. It's only just gone!"

And Vicky must have taken it.

Good luck, Vicky, thought Anne, as she walked slowly back to the disco. Should she tell someone? She could tell the others that Vicky had not been feeling well and had gone home early. But what about her parents? Then she remembered her promise to Vicky. Six hours' start. Her parents would be in bed by the time they got back to Usk on the last bus. She would tell them in the morning. By that time Vicky would be in Ireland.

---

suitcase, a case to put clothing for travelling in
harbour, a place on the coast where ships land

9

The ferry from Fishguard reached Rosslare at *dawn* the following morning, and Vicky had her first *glimpse* of Ireland. She felt quite excited, even though the harbour and the surrounding countryside were not as romantic as she had imagined. But things could only get better. The sky was clear in the west, and the *rising* sun was shining on the bright colours of the house fronts in the streets of the busy port.

Vicky lifted her heavy rucksack onto her back and walked down the *gangway* into the ferry building. Lucki-

---

dawn, the time of the day when the sun rises
glimpse, very short look
to rise, to get up
gangway, staircase or way out of ships for the passengers to get off the ship

ly there was no need for a passport when travelling to Ireland. It was only 5.30 in the morning, but there was a bus waiting for passengers from the ferry. It was going to Wexford, the nearest large town to Rosslare. Vicky asked the driver about buses to Cork, and he told her she would have to wait about an hour at Wexford. Vicky had wanted to phone the Matthews when she arrived in Ireland to tell them where she was, that she was safe, and that they should not worry about her. But the bus was ready to leave and it was far too early for a phone call. She would ring them later.

While she was waiting for the bus to leave, she looked again at her map. She would have to travel right across Ireland from the far south-east to the far south-west: 200 miles! And today was Sunday. There wouldn't be many buses. She would probably have to spend the night in Cork, the biggest town on her route, and travel on to Kenmare the next day.

Oh well, she thought, this is quite an adventure. If she had time, she would have a walk around Waterford, which the travel books had *mentioned* as an interesting town and busy port. She looked at her watch: 6 o'clock. The bus driver started the engine and they left the bus station exactly on time. Suddenly she felt very tired - and hungry. Perhaps she would have breakfast in Wexford instead of walking round the town. What she needed now was a little *nap* ...

Vicky awoke to find the bus driver shaking her by the shoulder: "Wake up, darling! We're in Wexford!"

---

to mention, to say, to state
nap, a short sleep during the day

Vicky sat up quickly. "Sorry. I must have *fallen asleep*!"

"Well, this is as far as we go. The bus to Waterford leaves in about an hour - unless you want to come back to Rosslare with me!"

"No, thanks. I've got to get a bus to Cork."

"You'll have to change at Waterford, darling," said

---

to fall asleep, to go to sleep

the driver, as he looked up the connection for her in his timetable. "You'll have a good two hours' wait for the bus to Cork, and you won't be there much before five-thirty this evening. It's an express service, but today's Sunday."

Vicky had breakfast at a small café in Wexford and caught the bus to Waterford. The people on the bus were friendly, and when Vicky told the young man sitting next to her that this was her first trip to Ireland, he pointed out all the interesting sights as the bus drove through the countryside and the villages. Every time they passed a church, he - and some of the other passengers, as far as Vicky could see - made the *sign of the cross*. Now Vicky knew she was in Ireland at last!

---

the sign of the cross, a sign made by Catholics: with their right hands they touch their head, heart and both shoulders as a sign of respect for God

10

Sunday began slowly at the Matthews' with the traditional "*brunch*". Mr Matthews was having breakfast in bed because of his broken leg, but Anne and her mother sat down at the dining-room table in time to listen to the ten o'clock news on the radio.

"Is Vicky still in bed?" asked Mrs Matthews.

"I don't know, Mum," said Anne *truthfully*. "She didn't come back with us from the disco. She left early. Perhaps she spent the night at her house."

Mrs Matthews looked up from her cornflakes in surprise. "You mean she isn't here?"

"No, Mum."

"Did she leave the disco alone or did she take someone home with her?"

"I don't know, Mum," said Anne, looking down at her plate of cornflakes. "I don't think so."

"I hope not! This is really very *naughty* of her! She's too young to spend the night alone, even in her own home. We're responsible for her while her grandmother's in hospital. You shouldn't have let her go off alone, Anne. You're older than she is. Where's your *sense of* responsibility?"

"I'm sorry, Mum, but I went to the disco to enjoy myself, not to *keep an eye on* Vicky. One minute she was there, the next minute she was gone!"

"I'd better ring her and make sure she got back safely."

---

brunch, a meal eaten in the middle of the morning instead of breakfast and lunch
truthful, honest
naughty, badly behaving, doing s.th. wrong
sense of, here: feeling for; taste, smell etc. are senses
to keep an eye on s.o., to look after s.o.

While her mother was ringing the number, Anne finished her cornflakes and buttered a piece of toast. What should she tell her mother? Nobody would pick up Mrs Griffiths' phone. Vicky would probably be half way to Cork by now. Vicky had had over twelve hours' start. Anne decided to tell her mother the truth.

Mrs Matthews came back to the dining-room looking worried. "There's no one at home, Anne. I'd better tell your father."

"Just a minute, Mum. I think I know where Vicky has gone."

"Gone? What do you mean?"

"You remember how much she was looking forward to going to Ireland with us, don't you? Well, she had a special reason for wanting to go. And that's where she's gone, Mum. She must have taken the Fishguard boat train last night. Paul saw her at Newport station with a big rucksack. She's gone to Ireland to look for her father."

"Her **father**?"

Anne told her mother about the letters Vicky had found, about her plan to find her father. Her mother's expression changed from surprise to shock, to worry.

"But **where** has Vicky gone. **Where**? She must have told you the man's name, the address..."

"She called him Brendan and he lives somewhere near Killarney. Honestly, Mum, that's all she told me about him."

Mrs Matthews looked at Anne as if she didn't really believe her. Then she went upstairs with more coffee for her husband. Anne went on with her breakfast in silence. A minute later Mrs Matthews came downstairs again and Anne could hear her on the phone in the hall:

"Hello? South Wales Police? I wish to report a missing person. Thank you." There was a break while the operator put her through to the right department. Anne went to join her in the hall. "Yes - missing since last night. Victoria Griffiths of 6 Wye View, Usk. She's just over fifteen and we think she's on her way to Southern Ireland - Killarney. My daughter says she took the boat train to Fishguard. Yes, we can come down right away. Goodbye."

She put the phone down and turned to Anne. "Get your shoes on, young lady! We're going down to the police station. I don't think you realize just how serious this is! If there's anything you haven't told me, you'd better tell it to the police!"

The *sergeant* at the County Police *Headquarters* was not as worried about Vicky's *disappearance* as Anne or Mrs Matthews had thought.

"You'd be surprised how many 'missing persons' - even kids - come home twelve hours later with nothing worse than a *hangover* or some story about spending the night with a friend!" he said. "But as you're quite sure that Vicky had a good reason for going to Ireland, we'd better contact the Garda - the Irish police - in Cork and give them Vicky's *description*." He turned to Anne. "What did your friend look like, Anne? Can you describe her?"

"Of course. She was about my height but a bit slimmer. She had black hair and blue eyes."

"Hmm. Anything else?"

"No."

---

sergeant, a police officer
headquarters, the main office
disappearance, the act of disappearing
hangover, headache after too much alcohol
description, explanation of what s.o. or s.th. looks like

"What on earth do you mean, Anne!" said her mother quite angrily. "Vicky has a long thin scar on her left cheek, Sergeant - from ear to chin. She got it in a car crash nearly two years ago. Her mother was killed."

"Do you *happen to have* a photo of Vicky, Mrs Matthews?"

"I didn't think to bring one. I'm sorry, Sergeant."

"I've got one," said Anne. "It's not a very good one.

---

to happen to have s.th., to have s.th. by chance

We had our photos taken in one of those machines at Newport Station a few weeks ago. Just for fun. I've got one in my purse."

"Thank you, Anne," said the sergeant as he took it. " - We'll let you have it back as soon as we've finished with it." He looked at the photo of the two teenagers in the small *cabin*. It was not a very good photo, but with her unusual *combination* of black hair, blue eyes and the scar, Vicky should be easy to recognize.

---

cabin, a little room e.g. on a ship
combination, mixture

11

When Vicky awoke the next morning, she had *difficulty* remembering exactly where she was. She was in a big room with about twenty other girls, and a bell was ringing loudly. Then she remembered. She was in a hostel in the centre of Cork, where she had arrived the *previous* evening.

She looked at her watch: 7.30! She was just about to turn over in the hard bed when a girl shook her by the shoulder. "Get up, or we'll be too late for breakfast! Mike's picking us up at ten past eight."

Who was this girl? Who was Mike? Then Vicky suddenly remembered. She had met her in the hostel last night. The girl's name was Patricia and she was a student from England. She and her Irish boyfriend, who was also studying in England, had come to Ireland by car a few days before. When Vicky had told her that she was on her way to Kerry, Patricia had invited her to join them - and share the petrol money.

They washed, dressed and hurried down to make themselves some breakfast. Half an hour later they were standing outside the hostel.

Mike was already waiting for them: "About time, too!" he said with a friendly smile to Patricia. And: "Who's this?" when it was obvious to him that his girlfriend was not alone.

"This is Vicky. She's going to Kenmare, so I thought I'd offer her a lift. She's offered to pay her share of the petrol," Patricia added quickly.

---

difficulty, problem
previous, the opposite of following

"That's fine, then. Come and meet Miss Moggy. She's just around the corner."

Miss Moggy? Who on earth could that be, thought Vicky. But Miss Moggy was not a person, she was a car. One of the oldest cars Vicky had seen for a long time. Miss Moggy was an ancient light blue Morris Minor Traveller, a *two-door, four-seater "shooting brake"* with a *wooden-framed* body.

"Isn't she *beautiful*!" said Mike enthusiastically.
- 'Beautiful' was hardly the first word that sprang to Vicky's mind. The car looked about fifty years old (it was in fact only thirty) and the paint and wooden frame

---

two-door, four seater "shooting brake", wooden framed, see illustration, page 50
beautiful, very pretty

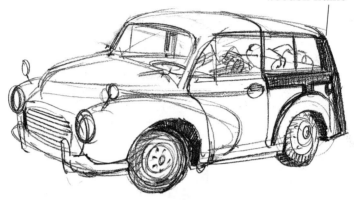

"shooting broke"
with two doors and four seats

were in poor condition. "I bought her in London for £300 last year. What a *bargain!*"

Vicky tried to look enthusiastic, but she was secretly wondering whether this old *jalopy* would get them to
5 Kenmare or whether it might not be quicker to walk. "You mean you've just driven all the way from London - in this?"

"Indeed we have," Mike went on, perhaps not noticing the note of *dismay* in Vicky's voice. "And she only *let*
10 *us down* once. We had a flat tyre soon after we left the

---

bargain, s.th. that is bought at a very good price
jalopy, an old car which does not work well and is not to be trusted
dismay, feeling of worry and discouragement
to let s.o. down, to fail to function

ferry. But *she goes like a bomb!*"

That was exactly what Vicky was thinking as she *squeezed* herself and her rucksack onto the back seat, which was already half covered with part of Patricia and Mike's *luggage*. Mike started the engine and let the *clutch* in quickly - much too quickly, Vicky thought, being used to her grandmother's careful driving. There were no seat-belts in the back either, so when Mike suddenly stopped at a red traffic light, Vicky fell forward against the front passenger seat, which lifted a little under her weight. Patricia gave a little scream of surprise.

"Sorry!" shouted Mike above the noise of the engine. "The brakes are very good, aren't they?"

They drove through Cork towards the road to the west. Conversation was difficult. Not only was the engine very loud, much of the luggage seemed to be camping equipment which had been thrown into the back of the car without any attempt to separate the metal items from each other. Some of the *rattling*, Vicky feared, might not even be coming from the luggage. It sounded as if the little car might indeed 'go like a bomb' at any minute. It was like riding inside a big, *old-fashioned sewing-machine*, Vicky thought.

---

she goes like a bomb, the car works very well
to squeeze, to push into a small space
luggage, bags, suitcases for travelling
clutch, you need to press the clutch pedal when you want to change gear
to rattle, to make a loud noise of pieces knocking against each other
old-fashioned, out of fashion, not up to date, outdated
sewing-machine, machine for joining two pieces of cloth, for making clothes etc.

"Did you *get* the tyre *fixed?*" she heard Patricia shout to Mike.

"What!?"

"The tyre...!?"

"No! Couldn't find a garage open at that time of night!" he shouted back. "But I think we'll be OK. The *spare* wheel looked all right."

So they were on their way to Kerry in a car that had no spare tyre on board. "How far is it to Kenmare?" Vicky asked.

"About sixty miles or so. We should be there in time for lunch. I know a short cut!"

For about an hour and a half they drove along the N22 through small towns with strange names like Ovens, Crookstown, Macroom and Ballymakeery. The country became quite *hilly*, and on the right Vicky could see high hills that reminded her a little of the Black Mountains in South Wales.

At Cloonkeen Mike stopped for petrol - Vicky paid - and took a look at the map. "This is where we turn left for Kilgarvan and Kenmare," he said. "It's only a *Regional road*, but it's much shorter than the National all the way to Killarney." The two girls took a look at the map and agreed.

The road climbed up into the hills and the little car began to get slower as the road got steeper. "Come on, Miss Moggy!" Mike encouraged. At last they reached the highest point and began driving down the hill towards

---

to get s.th. fixed, here: to have s.o. fix s.th.
spare, extra, not in use until needed
hilly, a landscape with many hills and mountains is hilly
Regional road, in Ireland: second-class main road

Kilgarvan. "Only about eight miles to go now!" shouted Mike. "We'll be in Kenmare in time for a pub lunch!"

But he was wrong. Just before they reached the village of Kilgarvan there was a bumping noise from the back of the car, and Mike began to *wrestle* with the *steering wheel*. "Oh no!" he cried. "Not another flat tyre!" He pulled onto the grass at the side of the road and they all got out. The tyre on the spare wheel which he had fitted two days before was as flat as a *pancake*.

"What now?" asked Patricia, although the answer was obvious.

"Pub lunch in Kilgarvan - if we're lucky!" said Mike. " - We'll phone the garage from there. *Cheer up*! Worse things happen at sea!" And with that optimistic comment he locked the car and led them down the road to the small village.

They had a pub lunch in O'Reilly's Bar, and Mike rang a garage he knew in Kenmare while the girls ate. " - Brendan's coming up with his *breakdown truck*. He should be here in about twenty minutes. Half an hour at most. Time for another *pint*, I won't be doing any more driving today!"

An hour later there was still no sign of the breakdown truck. Vicky was beginning to get a bit worried about *accommodation* in Kenmare. "Do you think there's a hostel

---

to wrestle, to fight using arms and hands
steering wheel, a car has a steering wheel for the driver to guide it
pancake, flat cake made out of flour, milk and eggs fried in a pan
cheer up!, be happy!
breakdown truck, a van used to take broken-down cars to a garage
pint, about half a litre of an alcoholic drink like beer
accommodation, place to spend the night

or somewhere cheap where I can stay?" she asked Mike.

"I'm not sure about a hostel, but there are plenty of B&B* places. We'll find you somewhere to stay. I'd invite you to stay with us, but Patricia'll be sleeping in our spare room - my parents are quite strict about things like that, and we're not even *engaged*."

"I thought you would be staying with relatives in Kenmare," said Patricia.

"Well, I **might**," replied Vicky. "But I've got to find them first."

"**Find** them? You mean you don't know where they live? They don't even know that you're coming?"

Should she tell her new friends why she had come all this way? She decided not to. "It's a surprise visit," she said, truthfully enough. "I got the address from my mother. They live in a small village called Templenoe. But I want to spend the night in Kenmare."

"Templenoe? I know it well," said Mike. "It's a tiny place. I might even know your relations. What's their name?"

"Sullivan," said Vicky before she could stop herself.

Mike thought for a few seconds before saying: "Sullivan? No, I don't think I know any Sullivans in Templenoe."

"It's a farm near the village. Long House Farm. Do you know it?"

"Never heard of it. But there are plenty of Sullivans in Kenmare. We can ask Brendan if he has any relatives in Templenoe when he comes."

---

* B&B = bed & breakfast

engaged, two people who promise each other marriage are engaged

"Brendan...?"

"Sure! Brendan Sullivan runs the garage I phoned in Kenmare. That'll be him now, with the breakdown truck at last!"

The door of the bar opened and a tall dark-haired man of about forty walked across to the small group of young people at the corner table.

"More trouble with that old jalopy of yours, Mike?"

The voice was deep, warm and friendly. He looked at the two girls and smiled. It was almost the same smile Vicky had seen on the photo he had sent her mother. There could be no doubt about it. She had found her father sooner than she had expected.

12

Mrs Griffiths was only *informed* of Vicky's disappearance on the Tuesday morning, when the doctors thought it would be safe to tell her. Mrs Griffiths had already asked when Vicky would be coming to see her again, so they could not *keep the news from her* much longer. They told her what they knew: that Vicky had gone to Ireland on her own, that the police had been informed and that they were doing all they could to find her. Mrs Griffiths took the news *calmly*. All she said was: "I expected this to happen." She didn't say why, but she didn't seem too worried either.

Two days later - on the Thursday after Vicky had gone to Ireland - Anne received a postcard with a Kenmare postmark. It simply said: "I've found him! Will write soon. Don't worry about me. I'm quite safe. Vicky."

"It's Vicky's handwriting all right," Anne said to her mother, who had already seen - and read - the card.

"We'd better show this to the police," said Mrs Matthews. "I don't think they're taking Vicky's disappearance seriously enough. She's been gone almost a week now. Vicky should have phoned us instead of writing. This really is too bad of her! Her poor grandmother will be worried to death when she finds out - and she'll probably *blame* me for not looking after Vicky better."

"I don't think she will, Mum. Not when she finds out why Vicky went to Ireland. I think she would want her granddaughter to find her father - if she knew where to look."

---

to inform s.o. (of s.th.), to tell s.o. a piece of news
to keep the news from s.o., not to tell s.o. a piece of news
calm, quiet
to blame, to say that s.o. is responsible for s.th. that went wrong

"Well, the police will know where to look for her now. And if they don't find her soon, I'm going to ring Joss at the 'South Wales Herald'. Sometimes the newspapers are more effective than the police - at least where missing persons are concerned!"

They drove down to the Gwent Police Headquarters in Pontypool and talked to the same sergeant, who happened to be on duty. He looked at the postcard, but he seemed more interested in the three pictures of Kenmare on the back. "May we keep this for the moment, Anne? Kenmare can't be a very big place, to judge from the photos. We'll fax a copy to the Garda there. I'm sure it won't be long before we find Vicky. In a little place like that they soon notice *newcomers*."

"I hope you find her soon," said Mrs Matthews. "My husband and I are very worried. After all, we're responsible for Vicky's safety. I was wondering if we should inform the press..."

The sergeant *frowned*. In his most official voice he said: "I would ask you not to do that under any circumstances, Mrs Matthews. The less *publicity* in cases like these, the better. We know what we're doing."

Mrs Matthews said nothing on the drive back to Usk, but Anne knew that she was not satisfied with the way the police were handling Vicky's disappearance. When they got home, Mrs Matthews spent some time on the telephone, and Anne could guess who she was talking to.

The next morning Anne got up early and made sure she was the first person to pick up the copy of the 'South

---

newcomer, s.o. who has only arrived recently
to frown, the opposite of to smile
publicity, if s.th. is widely known it receives a lot of publicity

Wales Herald' that was lying on the hall carpet inside the front door. Before her parents were awake she had looked through the paper from the first page to the last, but there was no news item about a 'missing Usk girl'. Perhaps her mother hadn't rung her cousin Joss, who was a reporter on the paper, after all. Anne was quite disappointed. But she needn't have been. The 'missing Usk girl' story had appeared in 'The Irish Times' that very Friday, just in time to be picked up and published by the local weekend papers in South West Ireland the following day.

When Inspector O'Grady walked into the Garda post at Kenmare early that Saturday afternoon, he was carrying a copy of the 'Kerry Post' under his arm. And he was not smiling.

"What the *devil* have you people been up to?" he demanded, as he burst into the office of the duty sergeant. "Haven't you read the papers yet?" He pushed the page of the newspaper with the short article *entitled* 'Welsh girl goes missing in Co. Kerry' under the sergeant's nose. "This girl's been missing for almost a week and the article says she posted a card to her foster parents from here! She's probably right here under our very noses! I want her found - today or tomorrow at the latest. If only we had a photograph of her..."

"Welsh girl?" The sergeant remembered the fax he had received from headquarters in Cork earlier that week. "I think I can help you there, Inspector. We had a Missing Person's Report from headquarters on Monday.

---

devil, the ruler of hell, the enemy of God
to entitle, to give a title to an article etc.

I think there was a photo *attached* - not a very good one, but at least something to go on. We had no idea she was in Kenmare until this fax from the South Wales Police arrived yesterday. I've got two men out looking for her now."

He showed the Inspector the two faxes he had received. The photo of Vicky had been *enlarged* but the black-and-white fax copy of the small photo was a poor one, and the face could have belonged to many young dark-haired Irish teenagers in the neighbourhood.

" - Arrgh!" *grunted* the inspector. "This is no good! It could be my own daughter Susan - or yours, Sergeant."

"I have three sons, sir!"

"You know what I mean. It could be anybody - and it was probably taken in one of those self-service cabins a couple of years ago."

"Except for one thing, sir. You can't see it on this fax, Inspector, but the girl has blue eyes and a long thin scar down her left cheek."

"A Welsh girl with blue eyes and a scar down her cheek! *Saints preserve us!*" cried O'Grady. "Where do you people have lunch? This girl served me a cheeseburger and coffee at that *fast-food place* here in the High Street only yesterday! A holiday job she said it was. Come on, Sergeant!" The two men almost ran out of the police station into the High Street.

---

to attach, to pin or glue s.th. to a piece of paper
to enlarge, to make bigger, to make larger
to grunt, to make a pig-like sound, to disagree
Saints preserve us!, idiomatic expression meaning you hope s.th. will not happen
fast-food place, restaurant where you can take food out or have little snacks cooked quickly

13

The fast-food restaurant was almost opposite Sullivan's garage in Kenmare's High Street. The owner had been very happy to give the young British girl a job for a few weeks during the tourist *season*. They were very busy at this time of year, and extra staff were not easy to find. One of his *waitresses* had left without *giving notice* the previous Saturday, so he needed an extra girl right away.

On his *recommendation*, Vicky went straight to Mrs Sheehan's *boarding house* in a small street not far from the centre of town and rented a small room for a couple of weeks. Old Mrs Sheehan took the money for the first week and asked no questions, for Vicky looked at least a year older than she actually was. Breakfast was included, but Vicky realized that she would not have much money left at the end of each week. It would not be long before someone came looking for her - either the police, the Youth Welfare people or - worse still - a very angry Mrs Matthews. How long could she expect to stay in Kenmare? A week? Two weeks at most. Long enough to find out more about her father. That was all she really wanted to do. She would not be able to stay in Ireland, and she didn't want to tell Brendan that she was his daughter. She just wanted to get to know him better.

The fast-food restaurant was just across the road from the garage, so she would be able to see him coming and

---

season, spring, summer, autumn and winter are seasons
waitress, a woman serving food in a restaurant
to give notice, to inform your boss that you want to give up a job
recommendation, information saying that s.o. or s.th. is good
boarding house, a place where one can rent a room for a limited time

going. Perhaps she could ask one of the other waitresses - or even the manager - about the garage owner and his background.

How surprised she was on her first morning when she saw Brendan leave the garage, cross the road and walk straight into the restaurant!

She walked up to his table to take his order. He recognized her at once: "Hello! Aren't you the girl who was in the car with Mike and his girlfriend in Kilgarvan yesterday?"

"That's right, Mr Sullivan. What can I get you?"

"A double cheeseburger and a side salad, please. And a large coffee. Are you over here on holiday?"

"Yes, just for a couple of weeks."

"And how do you like it here?"

"Well, I only arrived in Ireland on Sunday, but I love this part of the country already."

Brendan smiled. Vicky didn't know whether to smile back, but she could see the manager looking across at them. "I'll get your order," she said. And that was that. Brendan ate his lunch, paid at the cash desk and walked back across the road to the garage.

After work Vicky went for a walk around the small town and down to the river. Kenmare was like any other small market town in the south-west of Ireland. Indeed, it was like Vicky's home town Usk in many ways. The most interesting feature of Kenmare was the wide river at the south end of the town. Vicky walked down to the *quay* and sat on a bench, *gazing* across the water at Mucksna Mountain. The landscape also reminded her of South Wales, and she

---

quay, wall on the edge of a harbour
to gaze, to look hard and long

was just wondering whether she should not phone Anne to tell her she was safe and to ask how her grandmother was when she heard a *familiar* voice call out to her.

It was Mike. Vicky had not thought she would meet him again so soon. Nor was she prepared for Mike's question: "Have you been down to Templenoe to look up your relations yet?"

"No. Not yet. I've been too busy finding a job and a place to stay."

"Well, Patricia and I are driving down there this evening. There's a live-music *session* at O'Flaherty's Bar tonight. Would you like to join us?"

Vicky had to think quickly. Perhaps she could find out a bit more about her father if she went. But if Mike started asking people in the bar about the Sullivans of Long House Farm, she might have a lot of explaining to do. On the other hand, he would probably mention her anyway. Better to be there with him. Then she could face any *curious* questions herself. She wished she had never mentioned Templenoe, yet she couldn't refuse Mike's offer of a free lift. If Brendan no longer lived at Long House Farm, she would be able to forget about visiting her 'relatives'.

"I'd love to come! When are you leaving?"

"Nine o'clock from the market place. The session doesn't start until around ten, but all my friends will be there, and I've got a lot to talk to them about. Miss Moggy's back on the road again. Good old Brendan!"

"I saw him again today," began Vicky *cautiously*. "He

---

familiar, well known, recognized
session, a small, informal concert is a live-music session
curious, nosy, wanting to get information
cautious, careful

came into the restaurant where I'm working for his lunch. Does he live in Kenmare?"

"Yes. He's got a flat above the garage. He's been *separated* from his wife for over three years now."

"Separated...?"

"Yes. Their marriage didn't *work out*. There were no children, you see. So his wife went back to her old job in Dublin."

"No children?"

"No. That's one of the main reasons why marriages break up in Ireland. Brendan was really unhappy about it. He came from a big family and always wanted children badly himself."

"You seem to know a lot about him, Mike!"

"I should do. He's my second cousin on my mother's side."

Another relative, thought Vicky. Everyone in Ireland seemed to be related to everyone else!

"But surely he can get a *divorce* and *remarry*?"

"Divorce?!" Mike laughed. "This is Ireland, darling! We've only had divorce in Ireland for a couple of years, and in a small town like Kenmare most people are against it. Brendan is a brave man!"

"Why do you say that?"

Mike looked up and down the quay, and when he was sure that there was nobody near enough to hear, he said: "This is a secret, right? I'm only telling you because you're not a Catholic and you're not from Kerry. Bren-

---

to be separated, when a married couple do not live together they are separated
to work out, to be a success, to function well
divorce, legal ending of a marriage
to remarry, to marry again

dan told me that his girlfriend is expecting a baby in November. He's very pleased about it, but most of the older people in Kenmare will be very angry when they find out - if they can't see it already. Divorce is OK for Dublin or Cork, but they have different ideas about moral standards here in Kerry! Yes, Brendan's a brave man indeed..."

Vicky said nothing. So Brendan was separated from his wife. His first marriage was in ruins, and most people in this part of Ireland were against the idea of divorce and a second try! But if Brendan had always wanted children, the news about his girlfriend's baby was good news. He would have **two** children, even if he never found out about her! Vicky turned away and looked out over the wide river, thinking her own thoughts. She had almost forgotten Mike.

What on earth was the matter with the girl, Mike thought. Had he said something wrong? "Well, I must be going now. See you at the market place at nine. Don't be late!" And with that he walked off down the quay.

Vicky walked slowly back to the boarding house. She had never been to an Irish live music session in a pub before. What should she wear? She decided on her cleanest pair of jeans and a *fashionable* blouse which she had packed for special occasions. She put on a little make-up - mainly to cover the long scar on her cheek. Friends hardly noticed it, but strangers would. Then she sat down and wrote a short postcard to Anne. She had been meaning to phone all day, but still hadn't *got around to* it. She posted the letter in a letter box on the

---

fashionable, in fashion, up-to-date
to get around to s.th., to find the time to do s.th.

corner of the market place while she was waiting for Mike and Patricia.

They arrived at exactly nine o'clock and *whisked* her off down the street that led westwards out of Kenmare. O'Flaherty's Bar was already full of people when they arrived. The tables were taken, so they found seats at the bar. Mike seemed to know almost everybody in the pub, and it was not long before conversation turned to the visitor from Wales and her 'relatives' in Templenoe. Vicky was glad she had come. When the name Sullivan was mentioned, several pairs of curious eyes turned in her direction, but she was able to play down the original importance of her search: "They're not really close family. Cousins of my father's. They haven't been in touch for years, actually. All I had was the name Sullivan and the address: Long House Farm."

"The Sullivan family had the farm for years," said one old man. "But when the old mother died and Brendan, the oldest son, got married, the other children began to move away from home. They were only *tenants*, of course. They never owned the *property*. Brendan had problems with his wife. She was from Dublin and not used to the country. It's a hard life - always plenty to do and not much money left at the end of the day. The new Mrs Sullivan had her own ideas about how the farm should be run, and when things didn't work out, Brendan had to find a full time job at his uncle's garage in town. When the old uncle died, Brendan took the garage over. He had to give up the farm, but he's happy

---

to whisk, to take away quickly
tenant, a person renting a room, house or farm
property, s.th. belonging to s.o.; here: house and land

enough in Kenmare - or so I believe. The neighbours took over the farm, but they had no use for the old house. Only a big, long cottage really. They *let* it to visitors during the holiday season."

"Where exactly is it?" asked Vicky.

The old man took her by the arm and led her to a window at the back of the bar. "You can see it from here. That long, white building halfway up the hill."

Vicky could see it clearly. It was about half a mile away and looked very small at that distance. She felt she would like at least to walk up and take a look at it while she was here. Soon the live music session would be starting. She would walk up there now, before it got dark. So she said to Patricia: "I won't be long. Just going out for a bit of fresh air."

It was now almost ten o'clock, but the sun would not be *setting* for another quarter of an hour or so this far west. Vicky followed the path up the hill towards Long House Farm. It was, indeed, a long house. Just one *storey* of low rooms under a *thatched* roof that was in bad need of repair. There was a large Volvo parked outside the front door - rich *holidaymakers* from England, Vicky thought. She sat down on the stone wall near the front door and tried again to imagine what her life would have been like if she had grown up here.

The sun began to sink slowly behind the mountains to the west. Yes, she could imagine herself growing up here

---

to let, the landlord lets a room to the tenant
to set, the sun sets in the evening, it goes down
storey, floor, an apartment block with three storeys has three flats built one on top of the other
thatched, a roof covered with straw is a thatched roof
holidaymaker, a person who is on vacation

as a member of a family unit, but it would have been a different life, and she could not turn the clock back. Even if she told Brendan who she was, she would not make either of their lives any happier. He would want to
5 do things for her which she might not want and which

he might not be able to do in any case: he would soon be married again with a child of his own. He would not want to *adopt* Vicky now, to bring her to Ireland, to try to

---

to adopt, a child without parents can be adopted by foster parents

become the father he had never been. It was too late for that now. Vicky could only hope that he would be happy in his new marriage, and that her own grandmother would get well again soon. Soon she, Vicky, would be old enough to begin her own life. She had found her father, and that was the reason she had come to Ireland. She had seen the house where she might have grown up and could imagine the kind of life she might have had here. Would it have been a better life? Perhaps her mother had made a mistake by never marrying. Perhaps not. But it was too late to worry about all that now. There was nothing Vicky could do about other people's mistakes. Soon enough she would be old enough to start making her own mistakes.

"Anything I can do for you, love?"

Surprised, Vicky looked up and saw a *balding, middle-aged* English businessman *disguised* as a holidaymaker in Bermuda shorts, *sandals* and T-shirt standing outside the front door of the house. He was carrying an empty milk-can and was obviously on his way to the farm to buy some milk for his family's cornflakes next morning. What had surprised her most was his Birmingham accent, so like her own 'Brummie' accent before she had moved to Wales and lost it.

"I didn't mean to *intrude*," she said shyly. "But this used to be my father's family home, and I've come a long way to see it."

"From Wales by the sound of it!" said the Brummie

---

balding, losing his hair
middle-aged, between 40 and 60 years old
to disguise, to dress up so s.o. cannot be identified, to hide s.th.
sandals, light, open summer shoes
to intrude, to walk in where one is not wanted

with a laugh. "No disguising your accent, love!"

Vicky turned to go, but he called her back. He smiled at her, not wanting to seem unfriendly. After all, he was on holiday. He could afford to be friendly, even to a complete stranger. "Don't go without having a look around the place. Me wife'll show you the inside. I'm just off to get the milk. Lovely little cottage, but it must've been terribly cold in winter - and a bit lonely, too. You never lived here yourself, then?"

"No. My father left the farm when I was quite young."

If the *shrewd* Birmingham businessman noticed any *inconsistency* in her story, he was *polite* enough not to say anything. He walked off to the farm to get his milk, shaking his head, wondering why a pretty young girl like that should feel so attached to a place she had never lived in.

The sun had finally set behind the high hills and Vicky walked slowly back down to the pub. She could hear the wild sound of the folk music, and she suddenly wanted to be with other people, to be part of the big, happy Irish family inside the pub. She had seen what she had come to see. She would have a lot to think about over the next few days.

---

shrewd, wise in the ways of the world
inconsistency, s.th. not logical
polite, nice, friendly, showing good manners

14

Brendan Sullivan came into the restaurant for lunch every day that week, and Vicky always exchanged a few words with him when she took his order or cleared away the empty dishes.

One evening, just as Vicky was *getting ready* to go home after work, she saw Brendan come out of the garage, lock up and walk over to an *attractive*, red-haired woman of about thirty who was waiting outside. He took her arm and Vicky watched closely as they turned around and walked off towards the market place. She could not see whether Brendan's girlfriend looked pregnant or not, but they both looked very happy. Vicky was pleased to see that her father was starting a new life. It might be difficult to live with divorce in a small town in south-west Ireland, but life still went on in the usual way. She felt a lot happier now.

On the Saturday, while she was clearing Brendan's lunch dishes away, Vicky saw him make an unconscious *gesture* she was very familiar with: with the *index finger* of his left hand he was drawing the line of her scar along his own left cheek. Vicky dropped her eyes to the table and told him most of what she had been wanting to tell him ever since they had met: "I got that scar in a car crash. My mother was killed. I'm from a single-parent family, you see. I never knew my father. My mother and I used to live in Coventry. I live with my grandmother in South Wales now..."

---

to get ready, to prepare to leave or do s.th.
attractive, pretty, charming
gesture, a movement e.g. with the hands
index finger, the first finger next to the thumb, the finger you point at things with

When she looked up she was *astonished* to see that Brendan was *blushing* a deep red: "I'm sorry. I didn't mean…"

"That's all right. You should have seen it after the accident! It was much worse. The doctors did a wonderful job on it."

"Coventry? I used to know a nice girl from Coventry. I met her here one summer…"

Before Vicky could say any more, she heard Inspector O'Grady's quiet voice behind her say: "Miss Griffiths?

astonished, very surprised
to blush, to get a red face

Victoria Griffiths? I am a police officer. You have been reported to us as a missing person. I must ask you to come with me to the Garda post right away. If you have any personal property here, please collect it and bring it with you."

Vicky took the used dishes back to the counter, took off her *apron*, picked up her bag from the room at the back of the restaurant and followed the two policemen to the door. She turned at the door and took a last look at her father. He was gazing straight at her, an expression of surprise on his face. He had remembered that Jan had lived in Coventry. Had he remembered Jan's *surname*? He had certainly heard the inspector say it - twice. He lifted his hand in a wave of *farewell* and smiled at her. His *lips* moved: "Is he saying 'Goodbye' or 'Griffiths'?" Vicky wondered as she turned away for the last time.

---

apron, piece of clothing worn around the front part of the body when cooking etc.
surname, last name, family name
farewell, to say goodbye is to bid farewell
lips, opening of the mouth

15

"Do you think he knows?" asked Anne. They were sitting in the Matthews' garden in the afternoon sunshine three days later.

"I think he *suspects*," said Vicky. Then, changing the subject, she said: "Gran's coming home on Friday. Just for a day or two before she goes to the convalescent home for a month. The doctors say she should make a full recovery. I'm so glad! But I must clean the place up and do something about the garden. She'll have another heart attack if she sees that the lawn's not been *mowed* for three weeks!"

---

to suspect, to think you know s.th. without being sure
to mow, to cut grass

"Let me come and help you," offered Anne.

"No thanks, Anne. I'd rather be alone, if you don't mind. Tell your mum I'll be home by seven at the latest."

Mr and Mrs Matthews had been so happy that nothing had happened to Vicky that they had found it very difficult to be angry with her. Vicky's grandmother had taken everything *astonishingly* calmly, too.

When Vicky visited her in hospital her first question had been: "Did you find him?"

"Yes, Gran. I couldn't wish for a nicer father. And he's a happy man. Happy at his work, happy in private life, too." Vicky told her all about her week in Ireland.

Mrs Griffiths only had one other question to ask her granddaughter: "Did you **tell** him?"

"No, Gran. That's not why I went to look for him."

"Then why did you go?"

"To find out the truth. I feel much happier now. I can understand how Jan *fell in love* with him."

"Love...!"

"I know what you're thinking, Gran: love and marriage are the same thing. But it's not true. I'm sure Jan was happy on her own with me. She hated the idea of being tied down to one man. Brendan's marriage didn't work out, but he's found his own *happiness* with someone else. Maybe **she's** separated from a husband she couldn't live with, either. But they both looked happy in each other's company. And they'll get married soon and bring up a big family. Children - that's what Brendan always wanted."

---

astonishingly, surprisingly
to fall in love, to start loving a person
happiness, when you are happy you feel happiness, joy

Mrs Griffiths smiled and squeezed her granddaughter's hand. *Wisdom* from a fifteen-year old! Vicky was growing up fast. She had certainly learnt a lot about life in the last ten days, but she still had a lot more to learn, and one of the first things she would have to learn was how to drive a car. She would be sixteen next May, and Mrs Griffiths had decided to give her a course of driving lessons as a birthday present. The doctors had told her that with her heart condition she would probably not be able to keep her own *driving licence* after the age of 70.

Never mind, she thought. After her successful by-pass operation she was determined to live to a great old age.

With her granddaughter's help she would *make it*. What a fine girl Vicky was! So like her mother in some ways, yet so different in others.

Mrs Griffiths secretly felt very proud of Vicky.

---

wisdom, noun from wise, knowledge
driving licence, written permission to drive a car
to make it, to succeed in doing s.th.

Questions on the text

Chapter 1

1. The death of a single parent is only one way in which single-parent families can fail. What else might happen?
2. Are you for or against single-parent families? Give your reasons.
3. Single parents should have more than one child. Discuss.

Chapter 2

1. How do you think that Vicky's life will change when she goes to live with her grandmother in Wales?
2. Can you imagine something like this happening to you? Say why or why not.
3. What do you think Vicky's dream means?

Chapter 3

1. What do you know about Wales and the Welsh language and people?
2. Can you understand why Jan's parents were shocked when they heard she was pregnant? How have people's attitudes to this situation changed over the past years?
3. What do you think Mrs Griffiths' attitude towards her granddaughter is?

Chapter 4

1. What would you have done in Vicky's position? Would you, for example, have searched through the papers and opened Brendan's letter? Say why or why not.

Chapter 5

1. Why do you think Jan didn't want to marry Brendan?
2. What would you have done if you had been Jan/Brendan?
3. What do you think Vicky will do now? What would you do if you were in Vicky's place?

Chapter 6

1. Do you think that Vicky is "being a bit romantic" about the situation? Give reasons for your opinion.
2. What do you know about Ireland and the Irish? How does life there differ from life in Britain or in your own country?

Chapter 7

1. Have you ever looked forward very much to a holiday that had to be cancelled at the last minute? Talk about your feelings.
2. What do you think Vicky is planning as she waits for the bus on her way home from the hospital?

Chapter 8

1. Why does Vicky go to Newport on an earlier bus?
2. If you had been Anne, would you have acted differently when you discovered Vicky had taken the train to Ireland? What would you have done?

Chapter 9

1. Does religion play an important part in Irish life? What do you know about religion in Ireland?

Chapter 10

1. Anne doesn't tell her mother all she knows about Vicky's plans. What important pieces of information does she leave out?
2. What else do you think the sergeant at police headquarters could have done to find Vicky?

Chapter 11

1. How many words connected with cars and cardriving do you know? Who has the longest list?
2. Vicky meets her father very suddenly. What do you think her first impression of him is?
3. How do you think you would have reacted in this situation?

Chapter 12

1. Mrs Matthews says: "Sometimes the newspapers are more effective than the police". Do you agree with her?
2. Why do you think there was no story about Vicky in the Welsh newspapers, only in the Irish ones?
3. Where do you think the two Irish policemen are going at the end of the chapter? What do you think they want to do?

Chapter 13

1. What information does Mike give Vicky about Brendan? How do you think he got this information?
2. Why does Mike call Brendan "a brave man indeed"?
3. Do you think Vicky has done all she came to Ireland to do after she has visited her father's old home? If not, what do you think she will do next? What would you do next?
4. Do you notice any inconsistency in the story Vicky tells to the English holidaymaker?

Chapter 14

1. Do you think that Vicky's glimpse of Brendan and his girlfriend influences her decision not to tell Brendan who she is? Would you have done the same?
2. If Inspector Sullivan had been more tactful, the story might have had a different ending. Do you agree? Give your reasons.
3. How do you think the story will end?

Chapter 15

1. Why do you think Vicky "changes the subject" at the beginning of this chapter?
2. In what ways do you think Vicky's character has changed during the story?
3. What is your impression of Mrs Griffiths at the end of the story? Is she like a "normal" grandmother? Is she like your grandmother?
4. Did you enjoy the story? Is it a story with a "happy ending"? Does it have a real "ending"?
5. How would you have finished the story? Write a "final chapter" with your own ending.